me + you =

100 ways to work out
a formula for success

in your personal and
professional relationships

Maureen Bowes

Note for Librarians: A cataloguing record for this book is available from Library and Archives
Canada at www.collectionscanada.ca/amicus/index-e.html
ISBN 1-4120-8307-9

*Printed in Victoria, BC, Canada. Printed on paper with minimum 30% recycled fibre. Trafford's print shop
runs on "green energy" from solar, wind and other environmentally-friendly power sources.*

PUBLISHING™

Offices in Canada, USA, Ireland and UK
This book was published *on-demand* in cooperation with Trafford Publishing. On-demand
publishing is a unique process and service of making a book available for retail sale to the
public taking advantage of on-demand manufacturing and Internet marketing. On-demand
publishing includes promotions, retail sales, manufacturing, order fulfilment, accounting and
collecting royalties on behalf of the author.

Book sales for North America and international:
Trafford Publishing, 6E–2333 Government St.,
Victoria, BC V8T 4P4 CANADA
phone 250 383 6864 (toll-free 1 888 232 4444)
fax 250 383 6804; email to orders@trafford.com
Book sales in Europe:
Trafford Publishing (UK) Limited, 9 Park End Street, 2nd Floor
Oxford, UK OX1 1HH UNITED KINGDOM
phone 44 (0)1865 722 113 (local rate 0845 230 9601)
facsimile 44 (0)1865 722 868; info.uk@trafford.com
Order online at:
trafford.com/06-0062

10 9 8 7 6 5 4

Contents

Introduction
Acknowledgements

Thinking and Feeling
What's this book about?   i
The Process   v
Some Guidelines   vi
Why management is key   vii
What this book offers you   ix
How Self Development works   x

Doing
How to use this book   xiii
Your formula for successful relationships   xiv
Formula Lists   xvi
Name Your Pain   xxiii

What am I like?   xxv

20 chapters:

1. Knowing me   1
2. Knowing you   7
3. My Self Esteem   11
4. Your Self Esteem   15
5. Relating   21
6. Bouncing back   27
7. Passion   31
8. Setting goals   37
9. Being flexible   43
10. Being open   47
11. Being trusted   53
12. Trusting others   57

13. Can do   63
14. Expressing your emotions   67
15. Handling conflict   75
16. Give and take   81
17. Motivating   85
18. Forgiving   91
19. Intuition   97
20. Reflecting   103

What's my resistance?   107
References, Influences and Further Reading   113
Extra information   115

me + you =   119

Introduction

I've written this book as a tool to improve relationships.
Because people are important.....
and because you'll get where you want to be a lot faster if you can deal
with people effectively.

I'm a lifelong people watcher – the youngest of five children and
now, married for eighteen years, self employed and a mother of two.
Relationships are everywhere and they fascinate me.

Getting the best out of relationships, at work or at home, can be a com-
plicated and challenging process, so people often avoid going there
and just put up with one another.

My aim in this book is to reveal to you more about the *process* of relating, about what to take into account between you and another person,
so that you can make a genuine difference to the quality of your relationships and therefore to the quality of your life.

The most moving and inspirational experience for me is watching people achieve their potential. This book is my contribution towards you
achieving yours. I'd love to hear how you get on.

You can email me: maureen@peopleintelligence.com
I will reply personally to your email.

Maureen
www.peopleintelligence.com

Acknowledgements

This book wouldn't exist without the life, work and research of Tim Sparrow, Director of Learning, Centre of Applied Emotional Intelligence, and his collaboration with Jo Maddocks, JCA (Occupational Psychologists) Ltd. The framework is based on their model of *Individual Effectiveness* plus my personal learning.

The support of my husband and two children has played a crucial part in providing me with the right conditions and challenges for my growth and personal development.

Love and thanks to you.

John Hegley

I first came across John Hegley at the Edinburgh Festival in 1991, following up the Observer colour supplement's feature describing him as the alternative comedian's alternative comedian. I cried with laughter in that show. Back at work, I told everyone he was the best act of the Festival. Turned out my boss (Roger) knew him. My work involved developing awareness programmes in HIV/AIDS, which meant encouraging people to practise safer sex. Here was someone who could deliver that awkward message in a different way and reach more people. Roger arranged for me to have lunch with John and from that came the poem *French Letters: English Words* and the treasured verse:

Protection and collection
In those little rubber teats
Is something that can save your life
And also save your sheets.

© 1993 John Hegley

I lived in Edinburgh for four more years and enjoyed John's show at the Festival every year. I moved south and was out of the Hegley circuit for a while, then to my delight he came to our local Arts Centre. Inspired and elated I wondered if he could do the same for emotional intelligence as he did for condom use. And so here we have five of his poems for this book:

Minotaur	(1. Self Awareness)
The Boy and the 'Bad drawing'	(4. Your Self Esteem)
More drawing	(7. Passion)
Say it now	(10. Being open)
Talking about my feelings ain't my cup of tea	(14. Expressing emotions)

Special thanks to John, for connecting comic intelligence with emotional intelligence and helping me to reach a wider audience, once again, this time with EI.

Thinking and Feeling

What's this book about?

This book gives you a framework for how relationships work so that you can gain some insights and make some choices about how to develop your relationships.

Self

Let's start with you. How successful you are in your relationships is dependent on how well you know yourself (self awareness) and how well you manage your behaviour (self management).

e.g. You know you're always late and so you put extra effort into leaving 15 minutes earlier to be sure to get to your appointment, meeting etc. on time.

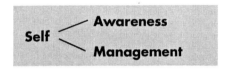

Other

Then there's the other person, or people, or group, or team. How successful you are with others is dependent on how aware you are of others (other awareness) and how well you can bring out the best in people in different situations (relationship management).

e.g. You calm down a group of nervous interviewees and help them to feel at ease while waiting for their interview.

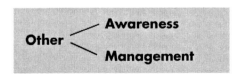

To increase your success in relationships, you need some know-how in all four areas, not just in one or two or three.

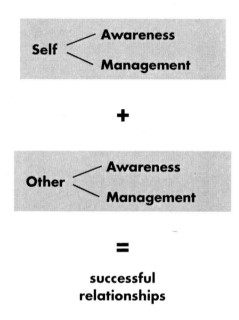

We can break down these areas into smaller chunks to make them more understandable and more doable:

Self   **Other**

Awareness

Chapter	Page	Chapter	Page
Knowing Me	1	Knowing You	7
My Self Esteem	11	Your Self Esteem	15
Motivating	85	Relating	21
Forgiving	91		
Intuition	97		
Reflecting	103		

Self   **Other**

Management

Chapter	Page	Chapter	Page
Bouncing Back	27	Trusting Others	57
Passion	31	Can Do	63
Setting Goals	37	Expressing Your	
Being Flexible	43	Emotions	67
Being Open	47	Handling Conflict	75
Being Trusted	53	Give and Take	81

Because we all behave differently in our different relationships, this book is designed so that you can create your unique formula(s) for success to suit your different relationships.

The Process – Action, Affirmation, Visualisation

The main content of this book is the twenty chapters giving you suggestions for how to improve your relationships. All are interlinked.

Each chapter has 5 suggestions for your self development. You choose one, some or all of these 5 suggestions.

Noting down your ideas, your insights and your responses to the questions, will complement the **process** and your **progress**.

Affirming goal

Each section has an affirming goal for you to repeat to yourself, silently, over and over again, for as long as you wish to develop that particular area. Affirming goals are intended to keep you focused, remind you of your focus and programme some encouragement into your thought processes.

Keep it going and notice how the habit conserves your energy and brings subtle changes over time.

Visualisation

Picturing your success removes doubt in your mind and heart, and changes your attitude. Each section has a visualisation exercise for you to practise seeing your success and, importantly, feeling your success.

The affirming goal and the visualisation are there for you to try something other than thinking to bring out what you've learned. The visualisation process will mean you can create some private space for you to shape your future.

The affirming goal means you can make progress even in your spare moments – you can repeat your affirmation while driving, waiting for people, going to sleep, anywhere.

Song lyrics

All our efforts through these sections have been captured by artists through different media at different times. I've selected popular and accessible song lyrics to reinforce the spirit of each section.

Some guidelines

- You'll get your best results if you **do** the suggestions and don't just read them.

- This means **taking time** over each of the suggestions you select.

- A nice, new **notebook** will help – writing or typing your thoughts and feelings, observations, reflections, insights and appreciations brings a different quality, depth and commitment to your development.

- Your level of **commitment** will determine your level of success.

The cause of difficulties in most relationships is ineffective or inappropriate communication.

If you could watch what happens inside you, in slow motion, when you communicate with someone, you would observe a process something like this:

stimulus

Can I see you in my office?

You **interpret** a meaning from the words, tone & body language.

This generates **feelings**

and **thoughts**

which influence your **intentions**

and your **response**.

Your response then becomes the stimulus to the other person.......and so it goes on.

Being aware of this process and managing it effectively brings impressive results.

It's easy to miss – either because you forget to apply what you know, and/or, because there's a gap of only a few seconds to apply it.

But this gap has huge potential for your success with others and is where self management / relationship management is most keenly tested. I refer to it as pressing the PAUSE button. This is what can happen if you do press PAUSE:

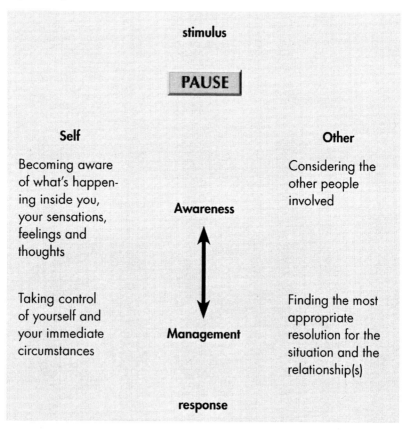

Your self management is what determines the results you get from yourself.
Your relationship management is what determines the results you get from your relationships.
This is a powerful formula for success.
Try it. It works.

What this book offers you

How we feel about ourselves and about others affects our performance. If we feel good, we get on well. Feelings affect our thoughts, our intentions, our attitude, our behaviour and our health. Feelings influence our actions – what we actually *do* and how we behave. Think how anger affects how you behave, or joy, or disappointment. This book gives you the chance to manage the emotional intelligence that has so much power, influence and potential in your life.

What difference does this make?

If you have successful relationships and manage your feelings well, you will tend to:

- Be aware of what's happening inside of you (your thoughts, feelings, intuition and your body's reactions)

- Take others into account

- Show respect for yourself and others

- Find appropriate expression for your feelings

This means

- You have a strong sense of personal freedom – not burdened by a backlog of unfinished business.

- You have peace of mind (and heart) – you have said what needs to be said, cleared what needs to resolved.

- You have self respect – you value yourself and others.

- You have emotional health – you are free of toxic relationships.

You can use this book as a catalyst to achieve these results.

One step at a time

We all have different responses to change. If the change is too big, chances are we won't go there through choice. Often though, we are willing to make small changes because these are more accessible and doable. So this book is full of small steps to change, which over time add up to real and lasting change that makes our journey really worthwhile.

Progress comes through change. We can all take one step.

Lasting change

The change will be longer lasting if you find your own answers. There are lots of questions here for you to find your answers to. And if you note them down, you'll be able to refer back to them, and learn from them, for years to come.

Best results

In personal and professional development there comes a point where we know we 'should' change, we know how to, we know that we can, but we don't. **Reading this book won't bring the change for you, doing what it suggests will.**

We have a choice with change. We can stay in a reluctant lethargy, or we can get on with it. It's simple really – we make a decision and we make it happen, steadily, one step at a time.

This book will have the best results for you, when you're at the point of determination, ready to dive in. Then you'll amaze yourself with the flow of the changes.

Let's not kid ourselves though, you'll only get great results from commitment and action. That means pushing yourself towards making things happen, not putting things off till another day. It means finding a level of personal discipline that works for you, so that you don't listen to your excuses.

You can get closer to the person you want to be. You can make it happen. So, what's stopping you? Go for it.................

Doing

How to use this book

Options

- Go to page xxv **What am I like?** and rate yourself on how effective you believe yourself to be with people. Your lowest ratings can direct you to your starting point.

- Start with the essentials – **Knowing Me, Knowing You, My Self Esteem, Your Self Esteem**, pages 1 – 19. These are the foundations of all relationships. All roads lead back here, so it's a smart move to start with these.

- Create **Your formula for successful relationships**. Turn to pages xiv – xxi of the introduction and design a formula to suit you on the basis of what you most want to improve or change.

- **Name Your Pain** on page xxiii and create your formula this way.

- Identify a specific situation where you're feeling stuck and complete a set of worksheets **What's my resistance?** on pages 107 – 112. Your responses will give you an overview of what's getting in the way and help you to clarify where to begin.

- Start at the beginning and work through to the end, or dip in and out, or pick the sections that are most relevant for you right now. This book is for your personal use, so be yourself with it. Use it in whatever way works for you.
  You can work alone and privately with it
  With a 'buddy' – a colleague or friend or partner
  In a group – your team or colleagues or friends.

Personal and professional development
Developing any of the areas in this book will improve your relationships – with yourself, with your colleagues, with your friends and your loved ones.

Knowing Me + My Self Esteem provide the essentials for improving your relationship with yourself. If you can do this, you will find it easier to face up to things without feeling hurt. The more you develop these aspects of yourself, the more you will welcome and value feedback.

Knowing You + Your Self Esteem provide the essentials for improving your relationships with others. The more you develop these aspects of yourself, the more your relationships will benefit.

We get our best clues about how to improve our interpersonal relationships from the feedback given to us or the criticisms made about us.

We can use this feedback to navigate away from the person we no longer want to be and towards the person we want to become – to remove our limits, to free ourselves from old behaviour patterns, to re-invent ourselves.

Like most people, you probably find it easier to name your 'faults' or 'weaknesses' than your strengths. Select the feedback you most easily identify with from the Formula Lists on pages xvi – xxi and let these direct you to create your formula for successful relationships.

Here are some examples ~

In her appraisal, Sue's manager praises her efficiency and organisational skills, as well as suggesting that she makes more connections with people, to become less distant from others, less independent.
Sue applied the formula for **Aloof.**

Paul dreaded his appraisal as he doesn't seem to hear any of the positives. He takes things too personally and dwells on what he could do better.
The formulas for **Sensitive** and **Unreliable** worked for him.

Craig's team joke with him about his direct, no-nonsense style. One day he overheard them saying what a slave driver he was and how he's not bothered about them as long as the job gets done.
He sought the formula for **Bossy.**

Tim's partner admits to being driven mad by his frequent critical and nit-picking comments.
He knew the formula for **Perfectionist** was his starting point.

Jenny's a worrier. She frets and gets bothered about things not going according to plan and not working out. It's just the way she is. She's not going to change.
She chose the formulas for **Controlling** and **Pessimistic**.

Formula Lists

Feedback	Formula	Page no.
Aggressive	Knowing me	1
	Knowing you	7
	My Self Esteem	11
	Your Self Esteem	15
	Expressing your emotions	67
	Handling conflict	75
	Relating	21
	Reflecting	103
Aloof	Knowing me	1
	Knowing you	7
	My Self Esteem	11
	Your Self Esteem	15
	Being open	47
	Trusting others	57
	Give and take	81
	Relating	21
Bossy	Knowing me	1
	Knowing you	7
	My Self Esteem	11
	Your Self Esteem	15
	Trusting others	57
	Being flexible	43
	Being open	47
	Relating	21

Feedback	Formula	Page no.
Controlling	Knowing me	1
	Knowing you	7
	My Self Esteem	11
	Your Self Esteem	15
	Being flexible	43
	Trusting others	57
	Give and take	81
	Can do	63
Critical	Knowing me	1
	Knowing you	7
	My Self Esteem	11
	Your Self Esteem	15
	Being flexible	43
	Forgiving	91
	Relating	21
	Can do	63
	Intuition	97
Emotional	Knowing me	1
	Knowing you	7
	My Self Esteem	11
	Your Self Esteem	15
	Bouncing back	27
	Expressing your emotions	67
	Passion	31
	Setting goals	37

Feedback	Formula	Page no.
Erratic	Knowing me	1
	Knowing you	7
	My Self Esteem	11
	Your Self Esteem	15
	Being trusted	53
	Setting goals	37
	Can do	63
	Reflecting	103
Idealistic	Knowing me	1
	Knowing you	7
	My Self Esteem	11
	Your Self Esteem	15
	Being trusted	53
	Can do	63
	Setting goals	37
	Being open	47
Impatient	Knowing me	1
	Knowing you	7
	My Self Esteem	11
	Your Self Esteem	15
	Relating	21
	Handling Conflict	75
	Give and take	81
	Reflecting	103
Indecisive	Knowing me	1
	Knowing you	7
	My Self Esteem	11
	Your Self Esteem	15
	Bouncing back	27
	Passion	31
	Setting goals	37
	Motivating	85

Feedback	Formula	Page no.
Insensitive	Knowing me	1
	Knowing you	7
	My Self Esteem	11
	Your Self Esteem	15
	Expressing your emotions	67
	Handling conflict	75
	Can do	63
	Relating	21
	Intuition	97
Judgemental	Knowing me	1
	Knowing you	7
	My Self Esteem	11
	Your Self Esteem	15
	Relating	21
	Being flexible	43
	Trusting others	57
	Intuition	97
Mistrustful	Knowing me	1
	Knowing you	7
	My Self Esteem	11
	Your Self Esteem	15
	Trusting others	57
	Being open	47
	Give and take	81
	Can do	63

Feedback	Formula	Page no.
Perfectionist	Knowing me	1
	Knowing you	7
	My Self Esteem	11
	Your Self Esteem	15
	Being flexible	43
	Forgiving	91
	Intuition	97
	Relating	21
Pessimistic	Knowing me	1
	Knowing you	7
	My Self Esteem	11
	Your Self Esteem	15
	Bouncing back	27
	Passion	31
	Trusting others	57
	Can do	63
Sensitive	Knowing me	1
	Knowing you	7
	My Self Esteem	11
	Your Self Esteem	15
	Bouncing back	27
	Passion	31
	Being open	47
	Expressing your emotions	67
	Handling conflict	75

Feedback	Formula	Page no.
Stubborn	Knowing me	1
	Knowing you	7
	My Self Esteem	11
	Your Self Esteem	15
	Being flexible	43
	Trusting others	57
	Handling conflict	75
	Forgiving	91
	Motivating	85
Unreliable	Knowing me	1
	Knowing you	7
	My Self Esteem	11
	Your Self Esteem	15
	Setting goals	37
	Being trusted	53
	Give and take	81
	Handling conflict	75
	Motivating	85

Name Your Pain

A different approach is to 'name your pain' and create your formula by identifying your source of unhappiness.

		Page no
Anger	Knowing me	1
	Knowing you	7
	My Self Esteem	11
	Your Self Esteem	15
	Expressing your emotions	67
	Handling conflict	75
	Forgiving	91
	Trusting others	57
	Reflecting	103
Low in confidence	Knowing me	1
	Knowing you	7
	My Self Esteem	11
	Your Self Esteem	15
	Passion	31
	Motivating	85
	Forgiving	91
	Trusting others	57
Guilt / regret	Knowing me	1
	Knowing you	7
	My Self Esteem	11
	Your Self Esteem	15
	Passion	31
	Being flexible	43
	Forgiving	91
	Setting goals	37

Jealousy	Knowing me	1
	Knowing you	7
	My Self Esteem	11
	Your Self Esteem	15
	Relating	21
	Being flexible	43
	Being trusted	53
	Trusting others	57
	Reflecting	103
Loneliness	Knowing me	1
	Knowing you	7
	My Self Esteem	11
	Your Self Esteem	15
	Bouncing back	27
	Give and take	81
	Being open	47
	Relating	21
Shyness	Knowing me	1
	Knowing you	7
	My Self Esteem	11
	Your Self Esteem	15
	Being open	47
	Relating	21
	Intuition	97
	Passion	31
	Motivating	85
Stuck	Knowing me	1
	Knowing you	7
	My Self Esteem	11
	Your Self Esteem	15
	Bouncing back	27
	Passion	31
	Setting goals	37
	Motivating	85
	Intuition	97

What am I like?

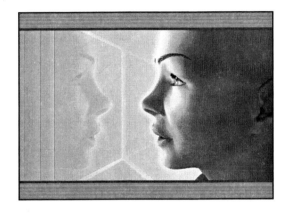

Rate yourself........

Here is a list of all the areas covered in this book that contribute to being successful with people. These involve *managing yourself* and *managing your relationships*.

Give yourself a quick rating to see how you think you're doing.

	poor	shaky	OK average	very good	excellent
	1	2	3	4	5
1. Knowing me I am aware of my thoughts, my feelings and my intuition. I sense how these network through my body.					
2. Knowing you I relate well to others. I see things from the other person's perspective.					
3. My self esteem I like myself, I accept myself. My behaviour shows that I respect myself.					
4. Your self esteem I accept and respect other people. My behaviour reflects this.					
5. Relating Other people recognise that I treat them as equals. I value others just as I value myself.					
6. Bouncing back I easily pick myself up and get on with my life after setbacks.					
7. Passion I have a 'can do' attitude. I make things happen.					

	poor	shaky	OK average	very good	excellent
	1	2	3	4	5
8. Setting goals I plan and review where I want to be and how I'll get there.					
9. Being flexible I am receptive to other people's ideas, suggestions and different approaches.					
10. Being open I easily make genuine connections with others.					
11. Being trusted I say what I mean, I mean what I say and I do what I said.					
12. Trusting others I am confident and clear in how far to trust other people.					
13. Can do I see opportunity or something positive in every situation.					
14. Expressing your emotions My behaviour matches how I intended to behave.					
15. Handling conflict I use conflict constructively in finding workable solutions for both parties.					
16. Give and take I recognise the importance of other people in my life and mine in theirs.					

	poor	shaky	OK average	very good	excellent
	1	2	3	4	5
17. Motivation I drive myself to perform in the way that best suits the situation.					
18. Forgiving I acknowledge mistakes, mine and others, resolve or conclude them, and move on.					
19. Intuition I know how to use different thought processes to guide my decisions and actions.					
20. Reflecting I review the effectiveness of my interactions.					

Now you can use your ratings to create a sequence for how you work your way through this book.

Do you trust the ratings you've given yourself?
Why not check out the ratings you've given yourself with someone else whom you trust and whose opinion you value. It's very common that the way we perceive ourselves to be isn't the way other people perceive us.
So how do we work out who's right? One to think about....

You can, of course, revisit and redo these ratings. It's useful to use a different colour pen and to make a note of the date each time you complete it.

20 Chapters

1. Knowing me

Every day a fantastic system in our body communicates to us via our emotions. We don't always notice.

The following steps help us to be more attentive to this intelligence at work and to translate those messages into appropriate action.

- Find where you feel your feelings
- Find your vulnerability
- Find your values
- Find your default mode
- Find your drivers

Affirming goal

I am in tune with my body.

Find where you feel your feelings

- Create a continuum ranging from feeling great to feeling awful.
- Across your spectrum of feelings note down what's happening in your body during those feelings, what your body does at those times.

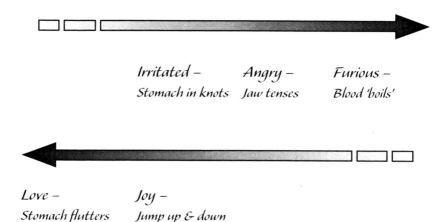

Irritated –
Stomach in knots

Angry –
Jaw tenses

Furious –
Blood 'boils'

Love –
Stomach flutters

Joy –
Jump up & down

- Create a journal and notice on a day by day basis what your body is telling you in relation to your feelings. Record this for a week to see what you can learn. It will give you lots of clues.

Find your vulnerability

- Recall recent situations where you have felt patronised, threatened, offended, put down etc., where you have not been pleased with how others have behaved towards you. Or situations where you felt very vulnerable.
- What was the emotional impact on your body?
- How did you manage your emotions and how your body felt at that time?
- What strategies do you have, when you feel vulnerable, to feel better again?
- Often the patterns we have create very short-lived periods of feeling better and can result later in feeling worse (too much chocolate, alcohol, cigarettes). Determine one constructive, nurturing, loving action that you can substitute for a more destructive, negative reaction, the next time your body feels that way. Something that reinforces your respect for yourself.

Find your values

- What do you value about yourself?
- Give examples of how you live your life by these values each day.
- If you find areas of inconsistency between the values you believe in and your day to day actions, find one thing you can do differently to bring your behaviour back in line with your values.

Find your default mode

- Think of people who have wronged you in some way.
- Write down the words you would use to describe your thoughts about and feelings towards them.

If the words you use to describe them represent for you avoidance of the person or situation, a concern about being rejected, not liked or disapproved of, the chances are you view your world from an *I'm not OK. You're OK.* position. This means you will tend to put your needs, wants and views second to other people's. This is likely to be your default mode.

If your words describing others in these more difficult situations represent for you a sense of sympathy for the other person, or an allowance for their behaviour (which covers your disapproval), or if you dismiss others, or feel judgemental, the chances are you view the world from an *I'm OK. You're not OK.* position. This means you will tend to put your needs, wants and views first, before the needs, wants and views of others. This is likely to be your default mode.

It's useful to be aware of this about yourself because it will colour your attitude towards others and they will pick up on this.

Find your drivers

- Which of the following statements most represents your approach to life?
  - *I need to be perfect. I strive for perfection.*
  - *I need to hurry up and get more done.*
  - *I need to please others and keep people happy.*
  - *I need to be strong and show no weakness.*
  - *I need to try hard – even if I don't succeed – trying hard is the most important.*
- What are the costs and benefits of this approach for you?

Minotaur

In the myth,
in the deep-down maze of the cave,
he went to find the Minotaur.
And before he went
he took a reel of twine:
a trick to traipse the return trip
back to the world of sense and sunshine.
It was sound thinking:
be enticed by new chance and challenge,
but keep in touch
with your place of origin.
Don't let your past be lost,
or it'll cost
your future.

Visualisation

Close your eyes and relax for a few minutes, just concentrating on your breathing until your mind is cleared.
Invite an image of you to emerge that you are proud of or that you like.
What does this tell you about yourself?
What can you learn about yourself from this and about how you are currently?

When you open your eyes, note down any actions you wish to take.

 Listen to *Beautiful* by Christina Aguilera

2. Knowing you

As we become more aware of who we are and how our feelings, thoughts and hunches affect our actions and behaviour, it becomes easier for us to read this in others and improve our relationships.

Walk the next steps in someone else's shoes.

- Watch people
- Notice
- Find the comfort zone
- Meet half way
- Find their drivers

Affirming goal

I perceive the world through your eyes.

Watch people

- Find an opportunity to watch a group of people around you from a distance, or with a sense of detachment – so that you don't get pulled in to their discussions.
- Watch how their feelings are communicated through their eyes, mouths, arms, hands and bodies.
- Note down the feelings that you can see or perceive.

Notice

- It's also useful to practise noticing – without judgement or opinion – just noticing:
  - *How comfortable people are in their own skin*
  - *How well they know their body and look after it*
  - *How well they know their own mind*
  - *How at ease they are with their feelings*
- How can these considerations enable you to improve your relationship with other people?

Find the comfort zones

- Draw your immediate circle of relationships, professional and personal.
- Observe each person in different situations.
- For each person identify
  - *What they are comfortable with*
  - *What level of challenge stretches them and*
  - *What level of challenge is too great a risk for them*
- How can these observations positively influence your behaviour towards them?
- What can you take into account when you're with them to bring the best out of them?

Meet half way

- From your observations of different individuals specify 2 or 3 things that you could do differently to accept and accommodate how they are.

Find their drivers

- Consider which of the following statements best represents different individuals' approach to life?
  - *I need to be perfect. I strive for perfection.*
  - *I need to hurry up and get more done.*
  - *I need to please others and keep people happy.*
  - *I need to be strong and show no weakness.*
  - *I need to try hard – even if I don't succeed – trying hard is the most important.*
- What are the costs and benefits of this approach for them?
- How can being aware of this improve your relationship with them?

Visualisation

Imagine yourself sitting with another person, whom you wish to know better or with whom you want to improve your relationship, in a relaxing, light and comfortable space.
You are both sitting with your eyes shut.
Experience your feelings and thoughts in that situation with that person and then, when you are ready, swap places and imagine the other person's feelings and thoughts in that situation.

Note down any insights or suggestions from this visualisation that may help to strengthen or develop your relationship appropriately.

 Song Lyrics

I wish I was your mother. I wish I'd been your father. And then I could have seen you could have been you as a child.

Ian Hunter

3. My Self Esteem

If we like ourselves and accept ourselves, we behave differently. We show respect for ourselves.

This section is about being OK with ourselves – a really important starting point for personal and relationship development.

- ❤ Move towards what's right for you
- ❤ Separate you from your behaviour
- ❤ Give yourself encouragement
- ❤ Make guilt a thing of the past
- ❤ Show respect for yourself

Affirming goal

I am creating a life where I value who I am.

Move towards what's right for you

- ❧ Note down examples of when you felt good, proud, successful, content, glad or at peace with yourself.
- ❧ What contributed to these feelings of valuing yourself?
- ❧ Identify some key pointers from this for how you are now and what it would be helpful to recreate in your life.
- ❧ Write down your decisions for how you will move towards making this happen.

Separate you from your behaviour

- ❧ Make sure whenever you use the words '*I am.....*' that they are followed by positive and constructive comments. Acknowledge anything negative as an aspect of your *behaviour*.
- ❧ *It was stupid of me to do that.* is more accurate than saying *I was stupid.* Believing *I behaved badly.* is more accurate than believing *I am a bad person.*
- ❧ Take something negative you say about yourself, or think about yourself, and rephrase it more accurately about your behaviour.

Give yourself encouragement

- Listen to the messages you give yourself.
- Replace any destructive messages with honest and encouraging comments.
- Substitute any harsh and untrue terms you use about yourself, like 'useless' or 'stupid', with honest and more constructive terms, like 'getting better at' or 'doing my best'.
- Programme your thoughts towards the positives about yourself and about your situation.
- Write down 2 or 3 constructive statements about aspects of yourself where you are usually critical or put yourself down.

Make guilt a thing of the past

- There's a valuable lesson in every mistake we make. What do you feel guilty about?
- Get clear in your own mind what you've learned from this and what good came out of the situation.
- Keep your focus on this and take this wisdom with you into your future.

Show respect for yourself

- Revisit yesterday – from getting up to going to bed, recall the things you did that showed respect for yourself.
- And then list your actions or behaviour that didn't show respect for yourself.
- Choose one item on your list that you can commit to doing differently, and in so doing, take one step towards showing more respect for yourself.

Visualisation

Recall a time when you felt relaxed and liked yourself or accepted yourself more than usual.

Get back in touch with those feelings as you relax and recreate them now through the power of your memory.

Enjoy how you're feeling and imagine your heart calm.

Retain this feeling, bottle it, label it 'Precious' so that you can access it whenever you choose.

 Listen to *Right to be Wrong* by Joss Stone

4. Your Self Esteem

When we disagree, make mistakes, are in conflict, or get let down, we tend to take a different stance towards the other person or party. And this attitude shows through.

Here are some pointers for remembering that we both count.....

- Find common ground
- Stand in their shoes
- See the other perspective
- Make the first move
- Spot the potential

Common ground

- To increase your respect for another person, make a list of at least 15 non-visible things that you both have in common.
- Now add the values that you both share.

Stand in their shoes

- Imagine the world through the eyes of others: what are their values, what drives them, motivates them, inspires them?
- Why? Increasing your understanding of why they behave the way they do, why they are the way they are, will help you to be more accepting of them.

See the other perspective

- See the situation you are in from the other person's perspective.
- Write down their perspective as if you were them, or say it out loud in the first person. "I feel….."

Make the first move

- Identify as many things as you can that the other person would appreciate you doing.
- Select one and do it.
- Take some small steps towards them.

Spot the potential

- In your relationship with this person note down your combined strengths.
- What potential does this hold?
- Note down your combined differences.
- What could go wrong? How could you prevent this?

> ## *Visualisation*
>
> Picture yourself with the other person, both of you ready to discuss your situation or your differences.
> Switch from your position to their position and voice your hopes and your concerns.
> See yourselves as unique and equal individuals who respect one another.
> Hear both of you saying something you appreciate about the other.
>
> Hold the image and retain the feelings into your relationship with that person.

 Listen to *Road to Acceptance* by Green Day

The boy and the 'Bad Drawing'

He said he'd made a mess of it
He told me he had scribbled it all out
I said, 'Please may I look at it?'
The pupil clutched his notebook and said, 'No.'

'Don't doubt yourself,' I said,
'Make more, not less of it.'
And the boy looked at the scribble
on the man
and he described someone caught
up in a tornado.
(Just like he was.)

© John Hegley 2006

5. Relating

It's easy to believe we treat others as equals. It's easy to have the words in theory in our head, but not necessarily in our heart.
Or our actions.

The following steps will direct you towards keeping more of a balanced attitude towards yourself and others.

- Know your rights
- Know your responsibilities
- Avoid judging others
- Take 2!
- Respect when under pressure

Know your rights

Take any book on Assertiveness. Near the beginning there will be a version of 'Your Bill of Rights'. This is a list of short sentences *"I have the right to......."* for example, *"......be treated with respect." "........state my needs." "........make mistakes."*
These reflect each individual's values and, when practised, influence their behaviour.

- What basic, personal rights do you believe in?
- Create your own list. Start each short sentence *I have the right to......*
- How do you demonstrate these rights in your behaviour with others?

Know your responsibilities

Any basic right that you apply to yourself is tested by how effectively you apply it to others. If you believe you have the right to be listened to, do you believe others have that right? If you do believe this, your actions will reflect your belief. You will listen to them. You won't talk over them or ignore their views.

- Go through your list of rights giving examples of how you put these into practice.
- Then give examples of how you demonstrate your responsibility to others by applying your basic rights to them.

Your personal rights and responsibilities could be referred to as your people principles. They are fundamental to how you demonstrate respect to others. They are fundamental to how you earn the respect of others.

Avoid judging others

We all have views, opinions, beliefs, political views and different life experiences. Our interactions with other people are coloured constantly by these. This means it's easy to make judgements about other people, to think well of people who share our views and to think less well of people who don't. *I'm right, you're wrong. It's your fault, not my fault. My way is best, your way isn't.* How we deal with these differences will affect the quality of our relationships and how we relate.

- Revisit some examples of differences you have had with other people.
- Link these to your rights and responsibilities.
- What could you have done differently for better results?

Clapper board – Take 2!

- Would others use any of the following words to describe you: patronising, self-righteous, passive, rebellious? If so, in what situations?
- Recall recent situations where you felt patronised, threatened, offended, put down by others.
- What could have been different? How would you have preferred to respond to get the best out of the situation?
- Does this respect both parties – with equal rights and responsibilities?
- Replay the situation(s) in your mind's eye, the words and the actions, to increase the chances of you behaving in a way that demonstrates your people principles in future.

(Check out Section 14 Expressing your emotions)

Respect when under pressure

- Pick a day that was particularly difficult for you recently.
- Recollect how you behaved with the people around you, especially those closest to you.
- Be honest, did you demonstrate respect for them? And for yourself?
- Write down what you've learned from this.
- What one step will you take to be more respectful next time?

Visualisation

Over a period of time take each of your rights in turn and see them in action.

Hear yourself saying the words that reflect each right.

Observe your behaviour, your actions, your body language, your facial expressions, that demonstrate each right.

Experience how this feels, managing your emotions to deliver your rights.

See others' behaviour towards you as respectful of your rights.

Feel this. Retain the feeling of being accepted and treated with respect.

Carry it with you.

 Listen to *We gotta talk* by Jennifer Lopez

6. Bouncing back

We all have bad days. Someone says something that upsets us. We make a big mistake. We forget something important. We can't find a solution to a problem. We get bad news......

The following suggestions reinforce that there is sunshine after the rain.

- Get this in perspective
- What's the worst that can happen?
- What's the best that can happen?
- Breathe!
- Rewind and fast forward

Affirming goal

I choose to show my inner strength.

Get this in perspective

- Be very clear of the facts of the situation. If you only have your perspective, write down what you know to be FACT.
- If it's appropriate, and/or for your peace of mind, find out other people's perspectives – the facts as they see them. Choose the best time, place and method for doing this.

What's the worst that can happen?

- We often waste time and energy worrying over things that will never happen. Think through the worst that could happen in this situation.
- See your worst case scenario from a global perspective, e.g. through the eyes of a disaster victim.
- Find what opportunities this situation is bringing you. What you might learn from it.
- Imagine yourself 3 months from now, 6 months from now. How will this situation appear then?

What's the best that can happen?

- Make a list of all the positive, possible outcomes from this situation.
- Choose 3 to steer you through the next few days / weeks / months.

Breathe!

- Find some space to sit or lie down and SLOW DOWN.
- Stretch and loosen your muscles.
- Take some deep breaths, in through your nose, filling your lungs and abdomen, then slowly (and noisily if possible) out through your mouth.
- Concentrate just on your breathing for a few minutes.
- From this physically more relaxed and energised position, tell yourself "*I can handle this.*" (See *References* Susan Jeffers)

Rewind and fast forward

- Reflect on other times in your life when you've got through setbacks.
- What worked then?
- Bring your success factors from those times into the here and now and add to these insight and wisdom from the person you have become.
- Keep this as an investment for the future.

Visualisation

See yourself surrounded by light that protects you.
Give it a colour (e.g. amber, turquoise, white).
Give it a shape (sphere, oval)
This energy field protects you by keeping negativity or anything destructive out. You only let in what is helpful and constructive to your growth.
Take it with you.

 Song Lyrics

*I get knocked down but I get up again.
You're never going to keep me down.*

Chumbawamba

7. Passion

The desire, the drive, the determination to make something happen.

So come on.......you can do it!

- Success comes in cans
- What's getting in the way?
- Watch your language
- Surprise others
- Make it happen!

Affirming goal

I choose to act upon what's important to me.

Success comes in cans

- How do you limit yourself?
- Identify all the times you say or believe *'I can't'* and question hard if and why that is true.
- List all the reasons why you can't.

What's getting in the way?

- Go through the reasons why "you can't".
- What is your interference here? What's getting in the way?
- Work out step by step ways to reduce your interference, to eliminate it and to prevent it, so that you can achieve your potential.

Watch your language

- Whenever you're about to say "*I can't*", consciously change it to "*I choose not to*".
- Experience the difference.

More Drawing

She told me I could draw. I said I can't draw, and she said
you can no more not draw than you cannot draw breath.

Surprise others

- How do other people limit you? Having explored how you limit yourself, consider how you allow other people to limit you.
- Bring yourself up to date with who you have become and behave as the person you want to be. It may take a little time but others will update their perception of you, if you manage yourself so that you don't fall into old patterns of behaviour around them. They will change their attitude towards you. Be patient though – others are not always as quick to notice as we might hope.

Make it happen!

- Identify what you would prefer to be different in your life/situation.
- Prioritise these.
- Mind map each of these areas to get an overview.
- Choose one area that you can take small, steady steps to progress.
- Schedule these steps over the next week to 3 months.

Mindmap of getting me + you = into print

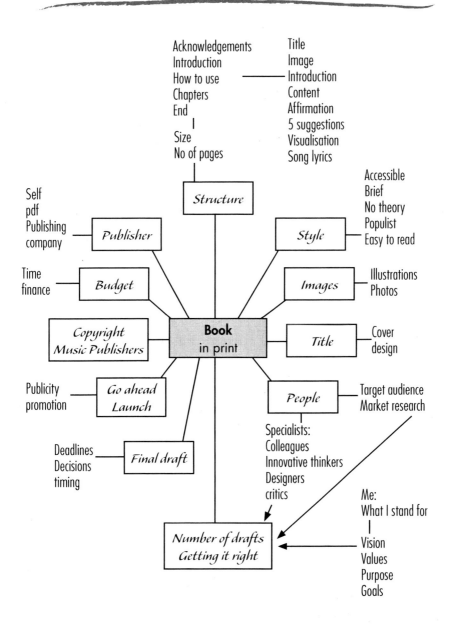

Visualisation

As you relax, repeat the phrase *"I can."* silently to yourself in the rhythm of your breathing.
Be alert to any images that come into your mind.
Select an image that you want to be a part of your life.
Keep remembering and revisiting this positive image.

 Song Lyrics

Take your passion and make it happen.

Irene Cara
(What a Feeling/Flashdance)

8. Setting Goals

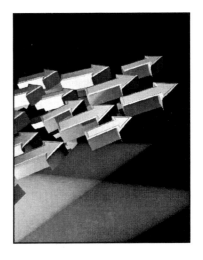

Achieving our dreams, our potential, our success, getting from now to where we want to be in the future, involves vision, planning, a positive attitude and pro-activity......

- Create a time line
- Prioritise
- Find your resistance
- Be alert
- Be accountable

Create a time line

Draw a line from 0 to 100 with you at the number of your current age.

- Note down significant events over the years and what you've done, or what has happened to get you to where you are now.

25	30	35	40	45	50

university   got   divorce
               married

started work   promotion   transfer

              Phil's accident

- Pick a realistic time frame for your future – 1 year, 3 years, 10 years etc.
- Get inspired. Generate masses of ideas – fun, wild, sensible and varied – for your future. Select a few good ideas to influence your future.
- Make some decisions about where you want to be / what you want to achieve during this time. Write these on your time line.
- Zoom in on this time frame and map out what needs to be in place for you to achieve your goals, starting now through to next week, next month, next 3 months, next year etc.

Buy house independently	Get fit & in shape	Travel to Australia 3 months
Decide on exact area	Join gym	Check HR policy
Save £500 per month	4 sessions per week	Budget for time out
Estate Agents listings	Stick to balanced diet	Network
		Tell Jo I'm travelling alone

Prioritise

- There will be many strands to your future.
- Be honest with yourself about **what** you need to tackle and **when** to achieve the results you want.
- Prioritise these to fit realistically into the timescale of your goals.

Find your resistance

- It's tempting to get on with the things we're good at, that we like doing, that come easily to us, while putting off the tougher stuff, the things we know we 'should' do but don't want to.
- Review your time line and be honest about how the tough stuff fits in there.
- Take the small step approach to managing this. If it's too big or too undesirable, you're not likely to make it happen.
- How can you break it down over a set time period to achieve the best results?

Be alert

- How might you mess up?
- What aspects of yourself could take over and prevent you achieving your goals?
- What triggers can you watch out for?
- Know yourself – intervene and prevent setbacks while you have control.

See example opposite.

Be accountable

- Let someone else know your goals, your plans. Tell someone your intentions.
- Commit to keeping them posted with progress updates.
- Write your commitment down and sign it.
- Take responsibility for making your goals happen – seek inspiration, seek others who inspire you.
- Keep reviewing your progress against your timeline.

Example – Be alert – Getting me + you = into print

- How might you mess up?

  I might put it on the back boiler and give priority to my immediate work that generates my income.

  I might stall on the boring administrative bits like getting permission to use lyrics.

  I might change my mind about paying to self publish.

  I definitely would stall at the process of going around publishers.

- What aspects of yourself could take over and prevent you achieving your goals?

  Being pulled by different priorities

  Being impatient and wanting things to move quickly

- What triggers can you watch out for?

  Self sabotage – allowing other things to take over

  How I schedule my time and priorities

  Asking myself Is it worth it? on the boring bits or effortful bits – Of course it's worth it!

  This is my priority – not other people's priority – this will mean waiting at times...

- Know yourself – intervene and prevent setbacks while you have control.

  Take small steps on the 'big' tasks or the 'boring' tasks.

  Make each small step a 'what I need to do next' step.

  Keep inspired.

  Keep my values and motivation to write this book foremost.

41

Listen to *My Way* by your preferred artist.

9. Being Flexible

We have choices every step of the way. We can dig our heels in and refuse to budge or we can move with what life throws at us.

- Loosen up
- No buts...
- Be different
- Flexible benefits
- Consider your options

Affirming goal

I am open to different options.

Loosen up

- Identify a situation where you were very fixed in your behaviour.
- How did others differ in their behaviour?
- How did their attitude differ from yours?
- What one thing would you be prepared to do differently in this situation that would enable you to behave with a little more flexibility and achieve a better result?
- Do it.

No buts.....

- List 8 different ways in which a non-critical attitude would enable you to be more flexible.

Be different

- Note down the times when you say *'It's just the way I am.'*
- Is it? Are you? Do you want it to be?
- If not, identify 3 small steps to start to become who you want to be.

Flexible benefits

- Think of two other people, whom you respect, and who approach things differently from you.
- What are the differences between your approaches?
- Do these different approaches complement or clash?
- Why don't you approach these situations in the same way?
- What stops you?
- What could you do or learn from them that would enable you to be more flexible in the future?
- How would this benefit you?
- How would this different behaviour or approach on your part benefit others also?

Consider your options

- Revisit a recent situation where your response was fairly automatic.
- Write down as many different ways as you can think of to tackle this situation. Not just the ways that you would tackle it, but all the different ways that very different people would.
- Genuinely consider some pros and cons.
- Decide on another option that you would consider taking in similar circumstances.

Visualisation

Identify in what ways you would prefer to be more flexible.
See yourself being extremely flexible and then feel your way around until you find how flexible is OK for you.
Enjoy the feeling of confidence in the level of flexibility you know is right for you.

 Listen to **Like a Feather** by Nikka Costa

10. Being Open

People need to get to know us before they feel safe with us.

How well people know us affects how connected they feel to us, levels of loyalty, willingness to go the extra mile and be there for us when it matters.

Here are some safe ways to open up to others.

- Be true to yourself
- Reciprocate
- What will people think?
- Privilege
- What secrets?

Affirming goal

I am open and honest with myself and with others.

Be true to yourself

- When/with whom do you pretend to be someone you're not?
- When/with whom do you hide aspects of yourself?
- When/with whom do you cover up something you've done or not done?
- Why?
- Consider your reasons and make some choices about whether you want to continue this way.
- Prioritise what you would like to change.

Reciprocate

- When someone tells you something about themselves or confides in you, reciprocate. Share something of yourself with them that shows you are listening, that you have understood and that you empathise.
- Another time, be the first one to share something about you.
- Create opportunities for you to reciprocate. Ask some constructive questions, empathise, share back from your experience.
- Record the difference it makes to your relationship.

What will people think?

- You tell me! Probably not what you think they'll think!
- Do you hold back on something you might otherwise share because you are concerned what others might think?
- Explore what they might think. And your reasons for believing this.
- What evidence is there for this?
- What would you think if someone shared the same thing with you?
- Why does it matter to you what other people think in this context?
- Why do you hold back?
- Work out how to say what you want to say so that others accept this and accept you. And so that you accept you.

Privilege

Sometimes when we disclose something about ourselves to someone, it creates stronger links between us because the other person appreciates us sharing our experience, particularly if this involves learning from mistakes, feeling vulnerable or uncertain. It makes us human.

Often people express gratitude when others confide in them. They certainly feel gratitude and sometimes privileged.

We benefit too because other people's responses enable us to put our experiences into perspective, to feel affirmed and to see things in a different light.

- How courageous are you when it comes to acknowledging your vulnerabilities to others?
- What lengths do you go to, to ensure a strong exterior?
- When do you hold back? What are your safe boundaries?

What secrets?

- Think about those aspects, details, thoughts and habits of your life that you haven't told anyone or that no one else knows.
- Re-evaluate them.
- How would your life be different if you were free of some these?
- If you confided in someone else? If you could just be yourself.

Things I don't talk to other people about:

Things I don't talk to other people about and would like to:

Say it Now

Don't hold on till it's time to go
before you let your emotional side show,
don't hold on until tomorrow,
don't hold on for another moment.
Saying I love you's not original
but nor is never letting someone know.
Why leave it till it's almost time to say the last goodbye
before you get to say the big hello?
Don't hang on till the gate is closing,
don't hang on till the daisies grow.
Why wait until it's nearly far too late,
why wait for another moment?
Do you feel at home with a heart that's hardly ever open?
Why keep it bottled up
when there's a genie hoping to get out
to shout it out,
the thing you really should have spoken about by now
why keep it bottled up until that heart is broken?
One wish: no feeling will dilly-dally.
One wish: no lagging with love to show.
One wish: don't be an emotional scallywag
or a silly so-and-so.
Say it now, it's not a moment too soon,
Say it now, don't wait until next July or June.
Say it now, don't wait for the next eclipse of the moment.
Say it now, give up on the muting,
Say it now, do a bit of re-routing,
don't go living in Slough
when you could be living in Luton
Town.

© John Hegley 2000

Visualisation

See yourself being open with others, protected and safe, without unnecessary boundaries between you.

 Listen to *Human* by The Pretenders

11. Being Trusted

Trust is the bedrock of our relationships. We all know how it feels to be let down and how it feels when we've let someone down.

The following suggestions will increase how much and how often other people trust you. And how much and how often you trust yourself.

- Take a second chance
- Trust you
- Your priority people
- Say sorry
- Know yourself

Affirming goal

I say what I mean, I mean what I say, I do what I said.

Take a second chance

- Think of recent examples of letting someone down.
- List the specifics of this.
- Clarify for yourself why this came about.
- How will you prevent this happening again?

Trust you

- Think of recent examples of letting yourself down.
- Specify why it happened.
- Clarify for yourself how to prevent repeating this – what specifically will you do next time you are in that situation to prevent a repeat performance.

Priority people

We cannot be all things to all people so being clear on our priorities is helpful here.

- Be clear:
  - *Who your priority people are*
  - *What your personal values are*
  - *How you demonstrate your integrity*
  - *To what extent these 3 areas are linked.*
- From these reflections, what are you going to do differently to be sure you get your priorities right?

Say sorry

- Whenever you recognise that you have let someone down, tell them you are sorry AND go out of your way to make sure it doesn't happen again.
- Think of one person or a situation that would benefit from your sincere apology and get really clear in your own mind and heart how to prevent future repeats.

Know yourself

How you behave and how you want to behave can be quite different things. To trust yourself, it's important to know yourself both as you are and as you want to be. If you pretend to be someone you're not, people, including you, will be let down.

- When do you act like someone you're not?
- What's the pattern?
- What action or small step can you take to prevent you acting and start being yourself?
- When will you start this?

Visualisation

Close your eyes and repeat the word 'dependable' to yourself.
Notice the images and the feelings that come to mind.
Think of someone you admire who is dependable.
What could you do that s/he does, that would make you more dependable?
See yourself making small changes and becoming more dependable in areas that are important to you.
See those people that matter to you appreciating the difference this makes to them.

 Listen to *Trust Yourself* by Bob Dylan

12. Trusting Others

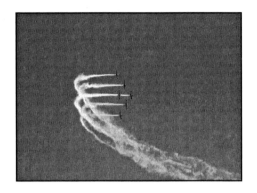

Some people we can trust wholeheartedly. Others, it would be unwise to trust. With most people, though, our trust builds little by little, as we get to know them more, and so learn how far we can trust them through their values and their behaviour.

These suggestions take you towards building or re-building trust.

- Give an inch
- Knowing me, knowing you
- A voice in my head
- Recognise the best
- In good faith

> ## *Affirming goal*
>
> **I am clear of how and why I trust different people
> in different ways.**

Give an inch....

- Identify the key people in your life.
- Where does your trust stop and start with each of them?
- What evidence do you need to increase your trust with different individuals?
- Where your trust is lacking, consider what steps you can take to build or rebuild trust – discussion, explanation, boundaries, accountability, new habits…..

Knowing me, knowing you

- Taking some key relationships, note down the behaviours and actions that have resulted in you trusting the people concerned. Behaviours that show their reliability, predictability and loyalty.
- Note down when you have felt let down by these people.
- Compare the two lists.
- What points can be made so that:
  S/he understands your needs
  You understand her/his needs
  You can both agree to start with doing one thing differently.
- Explain this in the context of getting the best out of your relationship and what the benefits would be for each of you.

Get to know your 'self talk'

The more attentive we are to our feelings, our physical responses, our thoughts and our intuitions, the more aware we become of the internal dialogue we have with ourselves. The more practised we become at stepping back and observing this dialogue, the more able we are to differentiate between the patterns and the games that we play along with.

Use the following suggestions to get to know your self talk.

- Think of a person whom you feel unsure of.
- What words, images or feelings occur around this person?
- What messages are whispered to you about this person?
- Be sure to separate these from what you want to believe or what you desire about the person concerned.
- Listen to your intuition. What's your hunch around this person?

Recognise the best

- People tend to live up or down to our expectations of them. So when they start to behave differently, make sure you don't crush their efforts with sarcasm or put downs.
- Whose progress might you have squashed along the way?
- What can you do differently, or make a conscious effort to say, that will show them you are pleased and keep a realistic level of optimism going?

In good faith

There comes a point in some relationships where we have to trust, we have to let go and believe the best or good enough.

- Recall some times when you have had to do this.
- What was your behaviour during the time of uncertainty, before you took the risk of trusting?
- What could you choose to do differently now and in future situations to manage yourself more effectively between uncertainty and trusting?

Visualisation

See yourself standing on a balancing board with the other person.
The board doesn't touch the ground as long as the two of you take
each other into account with your movement.
See yourselves taking confident steps as you move around the
board, considering one another and keeping balanced.

 Listen to *Trust* by The Cure

13. Can do

Is a glass half full or half empty to you?

Do you look to the good in every situation? Find the valuable lesson in every mistake? Search for solutions?

These attitudes and actions will take you towards where you want to be.

- Can do or Get real?
- It's all about attitude
- Dreams can come true
- Bring out your best
- One step at a time

Can do or Get real?

- Recall a time when you have suffered the consequences of being over-optimistic or too pessimistic.
- What were the facts of the situation?
- What was the cause of your over-optimism / pessimism?
- What facts were you missing to be misguided? What didn't you see, do or realise?
- What can you learn from this?
- What would make a difference in future so that you can 'get real' while believing you 'can do'?

It's all about attitude

In any situation you have to face, consider ~

- What's the worst that can happen ?
- What's the best that can happen?
- What's likely to happen?

Given the facts available to you, what's the best attitude or approach you can have for this situation?

Dreams can come true

- Describe the people you know who have made their dreams happen?
- What have the key factors been in their success?
- Describe the people you know who have restricted themselves through their fears and limitations?
- What have the key factors been in holding them back?
- What steps can you take towards your dreams and / or to remove a limit?

Bring out your best

- Do people share your optimism, become despondent from your negativity, encourage you or squash your enthusiasm?
- Who brings out the best in you?
- Identify why and how they do this?
- Is this the way you want it to be? What do you want to retain and what do you want to change?
- What can you adopt from this for you to bring out the best in yourself?

One step at a time

- It's easy to stay in the comfort zone of taking no action. It's easy to see our goals or our dreams as being too far away to come true and to leave them there. Far away. When have you done this?
- Some people only see their goals and bound along towards them missing out some of the steps until they trip. Any examples of this in your life?
- Our goals are so much more achievable with a balanced approach to one step actions. We can go fast or slow, but step by step we can reduce mistakes and move in the right direction.
- Note down some simple steps you can take to feel optimistic and move towards your goals now.

Visualisation

Picture people in your life, or famous people, who have achieved their goals. Observe how they look, how they behave, how they compose themselves, how they speak, their body language, their vocabulary, how they express their energy and drive.

See yourself comfortably transferring some aspects of their behaviour into your behaviour.

Say your goals out loud – with purpose and intention.

 Song Lyrics

Search for the hero inside yourself.

M People

14. Expressing your emotions

Do your emotions burst out with no holding back? Or do you sit on your emotions until, like Vesuvius, they erupt? There are many techniques for getting more in control of our emotions so that our behaviour matches our intentions. Here are some, but, techniques alone are not enough. The next pages are strongly linked to *Knowing Me, Knowing You, My Self Esteem, Your Self Esteem.*

- ❤ Accept your emotions
- ❤ Release your emotions
- ❤ Revisit
- ❤ What's your first feeling?
- ❤ Translating values into action

Affirming goal

I choose how I express my emotions.

Accept your emotions

How effective we are at expressing emotions will be determined by our experience of expressing them. Most of us could probably let out our true feelings with no one else around, however, we've learned our way of expressing emotions, in part, from other people's responses to us. Most of us will have been hindered by this and so have learned to be selective about how and with whom we express emotion.

We will get very different responses from people with the following life positions (See **Knowing me** page 3):

I'm OK. You're not OK.

These people will want your emotional expression to be over quickly, to sort it out, to snap out of it, as if it is wrong.

I'm not OK. You're OK.

People with this life position will also want your emotional expression to be over quickly but will manage their discomfort by saying things to help you feel better, or, by remaining distant.

I'm OK. You're OK.

People with this position will accept you and how you express your emotions. They will be there for you and support your expression until it's out of your system. And then you will both leave it behind.

- Consider different relationships throughout your life and identify those people:
  - *with whom you have felt wrong to express emotion*

  - *who have tried to 'make you feel better'*

  - *who have kept their distance*

  - *who have accepted your emotions.*

- How has this affected your behaviour and how you control your emotions?
- What is your attitude towards how other people express their emotions?

Release your emotions

Many of us have suffered from not letting go of emotions because we've become unsure of what's acceptable. (For example, consider what's acceptable to you about when, and with whom, it would be OK for you to cry.) If we don't manage our emotions effectively, they can niggle, torment, persist and generally cause discomfort for us because they need to be released. How much better do we feel for releasing them – talking to someone, sharing a problem or worry, going to the gym, punching a cushion or punch bag, cycling, laughing, crying, having a massage, writing ....? We are less effective with bottled up emotions, they slow us down, they trip us up, they affect our health and our immunity. Ignored for too long, they become toxic.

Accepting and letting go of our emotions takes a lot of practice for us as adults. Here are some simple steps to get started:

- Remember to notice your emotions throughout the day.
- Give the emotion a label, identify it. *I feel........................*
- Locate the emotion in your body – where is it?
- Be with it. Accept that it's there.
- Do some deep breathing and let the emotion go as you breathe out. If you find you are unable to let it go, welcome it as a call to action. Your body and your emotions are telling you to do something about it.
- Take a steady, step by step approach to freeing yourself of that emotion. What needs to happen? How will you achieve this?
- Plan what you will do to release your emotion naturally.

Talking about my feelings ain't my cup of tea

Please don't do the third degree
about the two of us
or the one of me
'cos I ain't one for talking about my feelings.
I just get these mental blocks
if it's insecurity the box it's in is ever so secure
with a very well-kept key;
talking about my feelings ain't my cup of tea.
Once when I had a nasty gash in my knee
and the doctor questioned me
about how I'd come to hurt myself
I was only too glad to be forthcoming
but enquiries about how I hurt myself
in the sense of self pretence and things like that
they make me want to flee:
taking about my feelings ain't my cuppa.
Anyway who wants to know
that someone thinks existence stinks
or that every day spent on this planet is one less day to go.
I'm not referring to me though,
it's just an example.
It's no big deal.
I keep my cards so near my chest
even I can't see the way I feel.
I used to be closer to my emotions
or maybe they were close to me.
In the past I've been very open
the last time was when I was twenty-three
months.
They saying bashing pillows is beneficial
and it helps to hug a tree.
They say problems shared are problems halved
but they don't say it to me
because revealing how I'm feeling it isn't my Darjeeling.

© John Hegley 2000

Revisit

- Revisit a recent emotional situation for you and note down how you expressed your emotion.
- Consider other options. What else could you have done? How else could you have expressed your emotions in that situation?
- Which option do you prefer?
- What can you learn from this?

What's your first feeling?

- Simply bringing up a subject can be a really difficult hurdle. To help you raise a difficult issue, think of some introductory phrases or sentences, that you could say out loud to get you started on expressing your more difficult emotions more comfortably, and that you could use to ensure you communicate them appropriately. It can be helpful to start the sentence with your first feeling – awkwardness, embarrassment etc.:
  I feel a bit awkward asking you this. I wonder if we can…
  I feel very embarrassed raising this with you….
  I'm unhappy about a situation and would really appreciate talking to you about it.

Translating values into action

- Revisit your values. (Page 3) How does the way you express your emotions demonstrate your values?
- What does it mean to express emotions honestly and with integrity?
- Think of examples from films, TV or real life of people genuinely expressing how they feel to the right person, at the right time and in the right place.
- How do people behave when they do this? What does this look like, sound like, feel like?

Visualisation

Think of a situation where you would like to have behaved differently.

Replay this situation in your mind's eye but this time as well as being the main character, you are also the film director, so keep redoing the takes until you are happy with your performance.

See yourself behaving the way you want to, hear yourself saying the words you want to, notice your posture, experience the feeling of expressing your emotions the way you want to.

Create a prompt – a symbol or word – to remind you to retain this feeling in similar future situations.

 Listen to **Shout** by Tears for Fears

15. Handling conflict

Love it, hate it, avoid it, look for it – conflict is what can happen when people express their differences. Handled well, it's a very healthy and constructive process on the road to achieving your potential.

Here you can review how you handle conflict and work out some ways for handling it even better...

- Making conflict constructive
- Be confident in conflict
- Find the right time and place
- Backtrack
- Do I really do that?

Affirming goal

I am confident in the face of conflict.

Make conflict constructive

- On a day to day, week by week basis, identify the conflicts that occur in your life.
- Which of these conflicts do you handle well?
- What constitutes handling a conflict well for you?
- Conflict is constructive when each person:
  - *explains the situation and their needs*
  - *listens to each perspective*
  - *problem solves*
  - *works out a reasonable solution that both can agree to.*
- What factors need to be in place for you to make conflict constructive?
- How does this differ with different people?

Be confident in conflict

- Identify any conflicts in your life that you would prefer to handle better.
- What factors can you transfer from those conflicts where you have confidence to these more challenging situations or people?
- What first steps can you take to put these factors into practice?

Find the right time and place

Many conflicts are made worse because we don't manage the timing, the place and/or our energy levels for dealing with conflict.

- Create some rules for yourself that you can stick to and that will help you to be level and assertive in conflict. (Think tiredness, think hunger, think anger.) It's amazing how very different a situation can seem with good energy levels and how much more effectively a conflict can be resolved.

- When you sense that the conflict isn't productive, suggest time out. Negotiate an agreement that you'll both pick up where you left off when the time (and energy) is right. Keep your word and stick to this.
  Give me 30 minutes to clear some important phone calls and then we can discuss this without being interrupted.
  Can we discuss this after lunch?
  Let's sit down somewhere else and talk this through.

Backtrack

- Recognise when conflict occurs in your life.
- Rewind or take a few steps back to just before the conflict peaks.
- What could you do differently at this point to prevent or minimise the conflict next time?

Do I really do that?

- Identify your strengths in conflict.
- And your vulnerabilities.
- Add to these lists other words that your colleagues, friends or family would say about you in conflict.
- Which words are you proud of? Decide how you will maintain this approach.
- Which words would you prefer not to be there?
- Identify a word that you want to erase from other people's experience of you and determine a small step approach to achieving this.

Visualisation

There is a popular poster and greetings card by Jean Guichard called *Phare de la Jument* (1989) which shows a man in a sweater and jeans standing outside the door of a lighthouse. All around the lighthouse the waves are crashing – easily 3 – 4 times the man's height.

There is a point of calm at the centre of any storm, at the centre of any emotion.
Imagine how it would feel to be centred in that point of calm in the storms in your life.
Centred in you.
Calm and confident that no matter how stormy things are around you, you will not be pulled into any destructive emotions.
You remain calm and in control on the inside, vigilant and connected on the outside.

 Listen to **Ordinary People** by John Legend

16. Give and take

When we reflect on how we got to where we are now, significant people in our lives form part of that picture.

These steps show us how we all count in our big picture. And theirs.

- Say thank you
- Interlink
- Belong to networks
- Find boundaries
- Ask for help

Say thank you

- Who are the people that contribute to your success? Or sense of worth? Or sense of achievement ?
- What is it about them, or what do they do, specifically, that contributes to this?
- Do they know this?
- Aim to communicate your recognition or appreciation of this, meaningfully, over the next month.

Interlink

- Write the names of all the people whose lives you contribute to.
- Then note down everything that you contribute to their lives.
- Keep extending your list as you recognise how many people's lives you influence directly and indirectly.
- Note your reflections.

Belong to networks and communities

- What are the main areas of your life that involve people?
- For each of these areas consider how you acknowledge and accommodate the wants and needs of others ?
- How do you ensure your wants and needs are acknowledged and accommodated?

Find boundaries

- Who do you welcome into the different roles in your life?
- Who welcomes you into their lives?
- Are you clear of where the welcome starts and stops? Of appropriate boundaries?
- Are they?
- Is there anything you could usefully say or do to show you will not go beyond that point, or, that informs others of the point you prefer them not to go beyond?

Ask for help

- What aspects of your life / job / situation do you find difficult?
- What would help you to make this a little easier?
- What could other people do to help with this?
- Think of a way to ask for help. Choose the most appropriate words to use.
- If you feel resistant, explore why.
- Keep on exploring why.
- Ask for help.

Visualisation

See yourself, surrounded by pure light, at the centre of your circle that interlinks you with all the people in your life. See the light steadily flow outwards from you, becoming stronger and brighter as it gradually encompasses everyone.

 Song Lyrics

Lean on me, when you're not strong, and I'll be your friend, I'll help you carry on, for it won't be long, 'til I'm gonna need somebody to lean on.

Bill Withers

17. Motivating

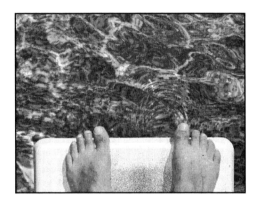

Motivation is about movement. Movement towards action.

Motivation is your self-drive, so you need to know what revs you up, what fuels you into action.

These suggestions are for discovering what moves you, what makes you tick, what moves your spirit into action.

- What revs you up?
- What moves you?
- Owe it to yourself
- Get your arse in gear
- And what about them?

All revved up

- Identify areas of your life where you are motivated.
- What are the different factors that fuel your motivation?
- Identify one area where you are not motivated but would like to be.
- What factors can you transfer from your highly motivated areas that would boost you into action in your less motivated areas.
- Plan how you'll do it.
- Programme it into your intentions.
- Create a visual reminder

What moves you?

- What gets you off your backside? Feelings, strong feelings, positive feelings or negative? Willingness to achieve or please? Desire for success or fear of failure? Discomfort from potential guilt? Necessity? Get to know yourself so that you can recognise the formula.
- What works for you?
- What needs to happen for you to make things happen?
- And then make some choices. Do you want it to be this way? What could change if you wanted to?

Owe it to yourself

- We are significantly more likely to deliver if we are accountable, if we commit to something out loud and then have to report back to someone.
- Create a check in process that would work for you that involves communicating with another person about your intended goal.
- State your goal.
- Make realistic plans for achieving it.
- List the small steps you'll take.
- Agree your check in times.

Get your arse in gear!

People sometimes express their inertia by sighing *I can't be arsed.....*
Great results mean *getting your arse in gear.*
Sometimes we just have to get on with it. No matter how much we want to dive in, the success formula isn't *wanting + standing on the edge.* No matter how much we want to lose weight or get fit, success won't happen with a formula of *wanting + sitting watching TV.*
We have to kick start ourselves and do it.

- In what area do you want to push yourself?
- Be honest, what's stopping you?
- How will you bridge the gap between wanting to and doing? What small steps will you take?
- How much does that achievement mean to you?

You're only a decision away.

And what about them?

- When people are flat and not motivated around you, what's your usual response?
- How do you decide how to respond?
- Different people need different approaches, different words, different styles to rev them up. What positive difference do you make to get them moving?
- What difference could you make to them?
- What difference could their enthusiasm make to you?

Visualisation

You have achieved your goal, completed the task, done what you needed to do. You are enjoying your reward. You feel satisfied, relieved and proud.

Revisit the steps you took along the way.

Remember how you pushed when it was easier to give in.

It was worth it. Look at what you've achieved.

Remember how you've achieved this.

Other opportunities and rewards can now come your way because you are free of this.

Value your efforts and your results. You've done so well.

 Listen to *Motivation Proclamation* by Good Charlotte

18. Forgiving

We can choose to live with grudges, resentments, hurt and pride for decades – and live with tensions and numbness.

Or we can choose to forgive – ourselves and others – and feel progress and freedom.

- Say 'I'm sorry.'
- Express your thanks
- Present or distant
- Find the intention
- Redirect your thought

Affirming goal

I forgive.

Say 'I'm sorry.'

- ❧ Say the words 'I'm sorry.' out loud.
- ❧ You can say them.
- ❧ Link them to a problem or difficulty you've had, either with yourself or another person.
- ❧ Reflect on what happened, from both perspectives, and what could have been done differently for better results.
- ❧ What part did you play? What could you have done differently that wouldn't have upset the other person quite the way it did. Be specific.
- ❧ Now turn that into a sentence starting with the words 'I'm sorry that I....'
- ❧ Commit to saying that sentence, sincerely, to the person concerned, when you're next with her/him.

Express your thanks

- Now you know the effort, emotions and courage involved in saying sorry, you'll have more empathy with others when they say sorry to you. This means you'll appreciate them for taking those steps towards you.
- Take some steps towards them to communicate your thanks that they've said sorry. A hug. A smile. *'Thanks for that.'* All communicate your acceptance and that you're both OK.
- You both feel good. It's easier to forgive if someone's said sorry.

Find the intention

- Sometimes very different behaviours, views and opinions come from the same (good) intentions.
- Reflect on your difficult situations and dig deep down to identify each person's true intentions behind their behaviour.
- The expression might be clumsy or inappropriate, but it helps forgiveness if you can recognise where they were coming from behind the words and actions.
  An angry *'Where have you been till this time?'* can really mean *'I'm glad you're back. I was worried.'*

Present or distant

Sometimes the person we want to forgive isn't in our lives anymore and we carry around a tension of unfinished business that may affect our other relationships and our ability to forgive others.

People don't have to be present to forgive them. You can still have a conversation with someone who isn't around anymore.

- Make some uninterrupted time for yourself.
- Reflect on the situation, the circumstances, the relationship.
- Note down the other person's perspective, what it would have been like for them.
- Note down your perspective.
- Forgive yourself – at that particular time and in those particular circumstances, you did what you could, with the energy and resource you had, you did what seemed 'best' to you.
- Acknowledge too, for the other person(s) – at that particular time and in those particular circumstances, they did what they could, with the energy and resource they had, they did what seemed 'best' to them.
- Say sorry to them out loud. Listen to how they might have said sorry today.
- Close your conversation appropriately – with a handshake, a hug…
- Let go.
- Forgive.
- Move on.

Redirect your thoughts

- When we feel wronged by someone, or when we've wronged someone, our thoughts can take us round in circles going over and over what's wrong. We pour our thoughts and our energy into something negative that preoccupies us and becomes a burden. What a waste!

- <u>Do</u> something. Give yourself a break.

- Discipline your thoughts away from this topic for a while towards something constructive. Repeat an affirming goal. Occupy yourself with other activities that engage you.

- Push yourself to move on.

- Then, with some distance and objectivity, decide what you need to do or say to leave this behind, to forgive or be forgiven.

- And do it.

Visualisation

See yourself as light. See your physical body as being billions of tiny particles of light energy. See everyone around you as being different physical forms of this living energy, the same life just different expressions of it.
See yourself as the same in essence.
See yourself moving on, untangled, unanchored, fine, free.

 Listen to **It's only love that gets you through** by Sade

19. Intuition

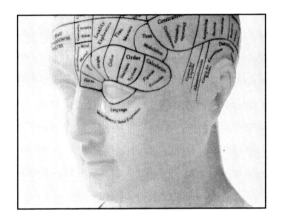

Gut feeling, sixth sense, a voice inside, hunch, the eleventh element, angels, guidance............

It doesn't matter what words you use to refer to this source of wisdom in your life, as long as you refer to it in your life.

- Pick up on 'things'
- Notice atmospheres
- Make space
- Scan
- Split second decisions

Pick up on 'things'

Our communication goes way beyond our words. Some of it is just below the surface ~ we communicate things we don't intend to, that move faster than our words, our bodies and even our thoughts.

- Remember some instances when you've said *'Something's not right here....'* or *'I have a good feeling about this.'* or when you've asked someone spontaneously or without obvious reason *'Are you OK?'*
- What was it that prompted your response?
- How did you know?

Notice atmospheres

- You know the kind of situation, you walk into a room and you could cut the atmosphere with a knife. The people are all doing what they usually do, if you took a photo the image would seem normal, but you just know something's not right.
- How do you know?
- It's well worth doing some kind of 'atmosphere check', as opposed to just keeping your head down, because many difficulties, problems, tensions, misunderstandings can be sorted through this type of awareness.
- Come up with 3 different opening questions that you could use in this type of situation to get you in touch with what's really happening and that allow people to open up. Avoid closed questions like 'Is everything alright?' Go more along the lines of *'You seem to be bothered about something ....What can I/we do to help?*

Make space

Our thoughts are quite fast but they are really slow when it comes to more intuitive or receptive thinking. The difficulty is that our day to day thoughts are often louder in our head than our more intuitive thoughts. These are more easily missed.

- To make the most of this faster, more subtle thinking, sit with your eyes shut and reflect on any situation where you're feeling stuck or unresolved.
- Be aware of your busy, noisy thoughts bouncing around, but don't follow these thoughts, step back and listen for the quieter prompts that guide you more effectively.
- Write these words or prompts down so that you don't forget them.

Scan

- Make a habit of scanning your thoughts like a radar.
- Step back from the chatter of your thoughts so that you are watching them, or hearing them as a neutral observer, with a degree of stillness. Scan and be aware of any other comments, thoughts, prompts or pointers in the background.
- These often provide real nuggets of insight. The penny drops, something dawns on you, what you've been looking for was there all along....
- Write these down. Trust them. Follow them. They're intelligent.
  Exercise some caution though. It's easy for strong feelings to swerve us into conviction. We can be absolutely sure something is the right thing to do, but really it's coming from desire. The real key – intuitive thoughts come from a detached and objective voice or guide. Be honest with yourself.

Split second decisions

- Take a decision you have to make.
- Without thinking about it, make the decision. Now. Without thinking about it!
- Now take as long as you like with criteria, consultation, research – whatever – and see where you end up. With the same decision or not.
- This is often what happens in interviews. You know within seconds who the best candidate is and then use the slower, systematic thinking process to validate your initial hunch.

Song lyrics

Intuition tells me how to live my day, Intuition tells me when to walk away, Could have turned left, Could have turned right, But I ended up here, Bang in the middle of real life.

Natalie Imbruglia

20. Reflecting

Something happens to our thoughts and feelings when we articulate them to others or just to ourselves, they become somehow more real, more powerful. We can make more sense of them, or simply accept them more, if we use the medium of communication to express them.

- Go for a walk
- Meditate
- Request some feedback
- Well done you!
- Revisit and review

Go for a walk

- By the sea, in the woods, in the fresh air, out with the dog…. wherever you choose to get some space, to be uninterrupted, to be in mother nature's lap, to let your thoughts and feelings run free, to be yourself.
- See what comes up.
- And yes, write it down.

Meditate

To think or reflect especially in a calm or deliberate manner.

- Sit comfortably.
- Close your eyes.
- Concentrate on your breathing.
- Ignore any other thoughts
- Do this for as long as it feels right for you.
- Scan your thoughts and feelings.
- Note down what you've learned.
- Repeat often!

Request some feedback

- It can be really heartening to hear how others have noticed you change, especially when they give you specific examples of how you handled something differently. It boosts you.
- So choose the right time and place and ask people you trust for their feedback or perception of you and how you're doing.

Well done you!

- Make a list of all the changes and developments that you've made.
- Rewrite each one so that it starts *Well done, ...(your name)....* *for......* and acknowledge, step by step, how you've achieved all that you have during this time.

Revisit and review

- Go back to any section of this book that you've spent time on.
- Read your notes.
- Get back in touch with how you were at the start, before you applied the exercises.
- Note down what's changed since then, how you feel now, what you're doing differently and, importantly, what progress you've made.
- Write a message to yourself for this date.

Visualisation

Recall a time when you were at your most relaxed.
Create a setting that suits how relaxed you felt.
Pay attention to the detail of this special place and to the detail of your relaxation – how your muscles feel, your facial expression, your breathing, the position of your body, the relaxing sounds around you.
Take in these details so that you can recreate and revisit this place to reflect, appreciate yourself and recharge.

 Song lyrics

I'm just sitting here watching the wheels go round and round, I really love to watch them roll, No longer riding on the merry-go-round, I just had to let it go.

John Lennon

What's my resistance?

Sometimes we feel stuck and don't seem to be able to identify why we're resistant to make a change or why we feel so uncomfortable about taking action. We put off phoning someone, we cancel a meeting, we don't finish a report. There's often no obvious reason why, we just seem to have lost the oomph to make it happen.

This worksheet is designed to help at times like these, it will help you to tackle your resistance by identifying its cause. This isn't a quick process but it will give you insights into what's getting in the way.
Again, personal honesty will bring you best results.

Briefly note down your area of resistance. Be very specific.

Now work through the questions on the worksheet.
Write down your response and give yourself an overall rating from 1 to 5, where 1 indicates very low effectiveness and 5 indicates very high effectiveness.
The high numbers will reveal what you are doing well, in your perception, the low numbers will direct you towards your top priorities for what to do about it, to make it happen, to get it to take shape, to move the situation on.

Your ability to respond to each question will give you some indication of where you are stuck and how to rate yourself.

	Ask yourself	Rating
1. Knowing me	In this situation: What do I actually feel? How am I presenting? / What behaviours am I demonstrating? Are there any patterns emerging – avoidance, delaying tactics, irritability, defensiveness? What are the feelings behind these behaviours? What's my hunch about what to do?	
2. Knowing you	In this situation: Who else is involved? What are my perceptions of their feelings? How does it feel from their perspective?	
3. My Self Esteem	In this situation: How highly do I value myself? To what extent do I accept myself here?	
4. Your Self Esteem	In this situation: To what extent do I value the other people involved? To what extent do I accept the others as individuals as distinct from liking or approving of what they do?	

	Ask yourself	Rating
5. Relating	In this situation: What are my rights and responsibilities? What are their rights and responsibilities? To what extent is my past experience with this person(s) clouding my judgement?	
6. Bouncing back	In this situation: How resilient am I? (High resilience means the situation isn't bothering you.) How able am I to pick myself up and move on?	
7. Passion	In this situation: To what extent do I feel in charge / in control? What opportunities does it present? What positives could come out of it?	
8. Setting goals	In this situation: How clear am I of the outcomes I want? And how to achieve them?	

	Ask yourself	Rating
9. Being flexible	In this situation: How receptive am I to different approaches or other ways of tackling this?	
10. Being open	In this situation: How open am I to others about the difficulties I face here? How willing am I to seek assistance or support?	
11. Being trusted	In this situation: How reliable am I in bringing about some change or committing to something new? What is the likelihood that I'll deliver?	
12. Trusting others	In this situation: How much do I trust others? How much do I trust myself?	

	Ask yourself	Rating
13. Can do	In this situation: What's the best outcome? What's the worst outcome? What outcome is realistic?	
14. Expressing your emotions	In this situation: To what extent do I accept what I'm feeling? To what extent can I let go of what I'm feeling? Am I free to express my feelings in a controlled and appropriate way?	
15. Handling conflict	In this situation: How well do I know my wants and needs? How well do I know their wants and needs? In what ways could we problem solve?	
16. Give and take	In this situation: How am I taking into account all the people involved, getting support and giving support?	

	Ask yourself	Rating
17. Motivating	In this situation: How can I find inspiration – for me and for them? What can I do to kick start myself? What's worked before?	
18. Forgiving	In this situation: Would an apology help? How can this be communicated? What are my intentions? What are their intentions? How similar are they? How positive do I feel towards the others?	
19. Intuition	In this situation: How well do I know the atmosphere or feelings generally about this? What's my gut reaction?	
20. Reflecting	In this situation: To what extent have I stepped back and consolidated? What would be helpful to reconsider or review?	

References, Influences and Further Reading

There are many people, many books and many theories that have shaped my work over the years, and therefore, this book. Here is a list of the main ones.

Back, Ken and Kate 1999 *Assertiveness at Work* McGraw-Hill

Burns, David 1990 *The Feeling Good Handbook* Plume

Carlson, Richard 1998 *Don't Sweat the Small Stuff at Work* Hodder & Stoughton

Carson, Rick 2003 *Taming your gremlin* Quill

Cherniss & Goleman, Editors, 2001 *The Emotionally Intelligent Workplace*, Jossey-Bass

Childre, Doc & Martin, Howard 1999 *The HeartMath® Solution* Piatkus

Covey, Stephen 1992 *The Seven Habits of Highly Effective People* Simon & Schuster

Dwoskin, Hale 2003 *The Sedona Method* Sedona Press

Gallwey, Timothy 2000 *The Inner Game of Work* Thomson

Gladwell, Malcolm 2005 *Blink* Penguin

Glouberman, Dina 1989 *Life Choices and Life Changes through Imagework* Unwin

Goleman, Daniel 1985 *Vital Lies, Simple Truths* Bloomsbury

Harris, Thomas A. 1973 *I'm OK. You're OK.* Pan

Jeffers, Susan 1991 *Feel the Fear and Do It Anyway* Arrow

Johnson, David W. 2000 *Reaching Out* Allyn & Bacon

Knight, Sue 1995 *NLP at Work* Brealey

Maddocks, J. & Sparrow, T. (2000) *The Individual and Team Effectiveness questionnaires. Users Manual:* JCA (Occupational Psychologists) Ltd, UK

Pease, Alan and Barbara 2004 *The Definitive Book of Body Language* Orion

Robbins, Anthony 1991 *Awaken the Giant Within* Simon and Schuster

Sparrow, Tim and Knight, Amanda 2006 *AppliedEI* Wiley

Stanier, Michael Bungay 2005 *Get Unstuck and Get Going* Box of Crayons Press

Extra information

The sections

The framework in me + you = is based on the Individual Effectiveness *ie* model of emotional intelligence.

ie is copyright JCA (Occupational Psychologists) Ltd.
http://www.ie-te.co.uk

The Individual Effectiveness Questionnaire has 17 scales. The chapters of this book correspond to the *ie* scales as outlined below:

Self regard = My Self Esteem
Regard for others = Your Self Esteem
Relative Regard = Relating
Self awareness = Knowing me
Other awareness = Knowing you
Emotional resilience = Bouncing back
Personal power = Passion
Goal directedness = Setting goals
Flexibility = Being flexible
Personal openness = Being open
Trustworthiness = Being trusted
Trust = Trusting others
Balanced outlook = Can do
Emotional expression and control = Expressing your emotions
Conflict handling = Handling conflict
Interdependence = Give and take
Self assessed EI = What am I like?

I have added 3 more sections to highlight their importance in effective relationships, but really they are facets of the other sections.
Forgiving is part of *I'm OK. You're OK.*
Intuition comes under *Knowing Me*
Motivation belongs within the self management scales.

The photos

These are royalty free from istockphotos.

The song titles and lyrics

There are song lyrics for every section. Those published are with the artist's or record company's permission. A title only indicates no response from the music publishers at the time of going to print.

Knowing You
I wish I was your mother. I wish I'd been your father. And then I could have seen you could have been you as a child. Ian Hunter
Used by permission.

Bouncing back
I get knocked down but I get up again. Chumbawamba
Used by permission.

Passion
Take your passion and make it happen. (Flashdance) Irene Cara
Used by permission.

Can do
Search For The Hero Written and composed by Mike Pickering/Paul Heard
Published by BMG Music Publishing Ltd. Used by permission

Give and take
Lean on me (Withers) Universal/MCA Music Limited.

Intuition
Intuition Natalie Imbruglia
Published by BMG Music Publishing Ltd.

Reflecting
Watching the wheels John Lennon
Hal Leonard Corporation.

116

Poems by John Hegley

1. Knowing me
Minotaur *Uncut Confetti* 2006 Methuen

4. Your Self Esteem
The boy and the 'Bad Drawing' © John Hegley 2006

7. Passion
More drawing *Dog* 2000 Methuen

10. Being Open
Say it now *Dog* 2000 Methuen

14. Expressing your emotions
Talking about my feelings ain't my cup of tea
Five sugars please 1993 Methuen

me + you = ?

excitement?
stability?
a good job well done?
wonder?
hope?
creativity?
action?
results?
love?
camaraderie?
loyalty?
friendship?
commitment?
opportunity?
integrity?
teamwork?
excitement?
goals?
fun?
innovation?
adventure?
laughter?
achievement?
respect?
fulfillment?
safety?
responsibility?
enthusiasm?
happiness?

ISBN 141208307-9

9 781412 083072